Hawaiian Cookbook

Kelly Malone
Georgianna Lagoria

ILLUSTRATED BY
MARY MURPHY

First published in 1994 by
The Appletree Press Ltd,
19–21 Alfred Street,
Belfast BT2 8DL
Tel: +44 232 243 074 Fax: +44 232 246 756

A Little Hawaiian Cookbook

First published in the United States in 1994 by
Chronicle Books, 275 Fifth Street,
San Francisco, CA 94103

ISBN 0-8118-0642-1

9 8 7 6 5 4 3 2 1

Introduction

The Hawaiian Islands are unique in their beauty and cultural diversity. Formed by volcanoes, the still-evolving landscape stretches from glistening beaches up through cool green valleys and higher still to the rugged cliffs named *pali* by the Hawaiians.

The native Pacific Islanders, who first populated Hawaii, introduced foods such as roasted pig, taro *poi*, and coconut. All of these are still associated with the traditional *luau* feast, a custom kept very much alive through Hawaiian family celebrations and the more commercial *luaus* offered to tourists.

Located in the center of the Pacific Ocean, the islands have also attracted a lively mix of peoples including mainland Americans, Chinese, Filipinos, Japanese, Koreans, Portuguese and Puerto Ricans, each bringing a knowledge of and preference for certain ways of living and eating. This cultural medley, added to the tropical climate and the relaxed informality of the local people, has resulted in a varied and distinctive cuisine.

A note on measures

Unless stated otherwise, each recipe serves four. Where classic ingredients may be hard to find, more commonly available substitutes have been recommended.

Lomi Lomi Salmon in Cherry Tomatoes

The missionaries had a preference for salted fish over fresh fish and developed this dish, now a staple at *luaus*. In Hawaiian, the word *lomi* means to crush or massage. The fish is soaked to remove the salt, then "massaged" (mashed with the fingers) to break it apart. Like most *malahini*, or newcomers, to the Islands, we had our first taste of *lomi* salmon at a hotel *luau*, where we were encouraged to alternate bites of the fish with fingers of rich, earthy *poi*. Stuffed in cherry tomatoes, *lomi* salmon makes a tempting appetizer or, as the Hawaiians say, *pupu*.

---

6 oz salt salmon
1 yellow onion, peeled and chopped
1 large tomato, finely diced
1 1/2 green onions, finely chopped
16 firm, ripe, cherry tomatoes, washed (not too small)
(makes 16 appetizers)

Soak the salmon in water for 1 hour. If the salmon is too salty, soak for another hour. Remove the skin and bones. Place in a mixing bowl and mash the salmon between the fingers. Add diced tomato and two-thirds of the onions. Chill mixture for 2 hours. Slice a thin piece from the bottom of each cherry tomato, making it flat, so it will stand without tipping over. Hollow the tomatoes and refrigerate until ready to use. When the *lomi* salmon is ready, fill the tomatoes and garnish with a sprinkle of the remaining onions.

If you want to substitute fresh salmon, marinate it in 1/2 cup lime juice instead of soaking in the water. For a spicier version add a pinch of white pepper and a few drops of Tabasco.

Poke

Poke (pronounced "pokay") is a close relative to *sashimi* (carefully sliced raw fish) brought by Japanese immigrants to Hawaii. An everyday favorite of locals, *poke* can be purchased already prepared in markets, fast-food, and fish shops all over the Islands. Many varieties of fish can be used including raw and boiled tuna, and sliced octopus, which Hawaiian cooks mix with strands of crunchy, edible seaweed.

---

*$1/2$ lb fresh white fish (cod, snapper, halibut, etc.)
cleaned, skinned, boned, and cut into $1/2$ inch cubes
$1/2$ cup chopped white onion
2 green onions, trimmed and chopped
$1/2$ inch piece fresh ginger root, peeled and grated
$1/2$ tsp hot chili oil (available in Asian markets)
(or a few drops of Tabasco and 1 tsp peanut oil)
2 tsp soy sauce
salt to taste*

Combine all ingredients and refrigerate. Serve chilled.

Grilled Shrimp and Pineapple

Hawaiians love barbecues. On Sunday afternoons, the sound of laughter and the scent of meat, basted in soy grilling sauces, mix with the salty sea air. In the 1950s, when backyard *luaus* became fashionable, the art of barbecuing underwent a renaissance. Table-top cooking became the rage. *Pupus* (like these kebabs) were often charred over a can of Sterno-fuel and placed in a hollowed-out pineapple. For health and safety reasons, we recommend a grill!

---

¹/₂ cup soy sauce
¹/₄ cup sugar
¹/₄ inch slice fresh ginger root, peeled and grated
1¹/₂ cups pineapple juice
¹/₃ cup fresh lime juice
2 lbs large cooked prawns (32 pieces),
peeled and deveined
2 large pineapples, peeled, cored and cut into 1 inch cubes
2 green peppers, de-seeded and cut into 1 inch dice
16 metal or bamboo skewers
(makes 16 kebabs)

If you are using bamboo skewers, soak them in water for 24 hours to reduce the chance of the sticks burning on the fire. In a large saucepan, heat soy sauce, sugar, ginger, pineapple juice, and lime juice. Simmer for five minutes. On each skewer — alternating ingredients — thread two prawns, two pineapple cubes and two pieces of green pepper. Brush with sauce and grill until browned for about 4 minutes, turning once. Serve with remaining sauce for dipping.

Gri... ...fish

Fish and seaweed... ...and happiness to the
Japanese, whose... ...felt in many areas of
Hawaiian life. W... ...ddhism, which required
a vegetarian di... ...ed many recipes using
alternatives to... ...(Japanese soy sauce), the
base for teriyak...

> 4... ...firm white fish
> 4... ...(see below)

Arrange fish in a large baking pan and cover with sauce. Marinate for
3–4 hours. Remove from marinade and grill or barbecue fish, turning
once, until the flesh flakes easily with a fork.

Teriyaki Sauce

Teriyaki is a sweet and salty sauce used to marinate chicken, fish, and
beef before grilling or broiling.

1 cup soy sauce	2 tbsp sherry
1/3 cup sugar	1 tbsp toasted sesame seeds
2 garlic cloves, peeled and crushed	1/4 cup sliced green onions
1/2 inch piece fresh ginger root, peeled and grated	

Mix all the ingredients together and store in a small bowl in the
refrigerator for up to three weeks.

Coconut Baked Fish

Originally, Hawaiians used three cooking methods: coal-roasting, pit-smoking, or boiling. Because they did not have heavy pots, they boiled their food by tossing fire-heated rocks into the bowls of liquid. Their original methods for cooking may be more romantic, but today we prefer to use modern appliances. This recipe incorporates foods introduced by the Portuguese, Chinese, and Puerto Rican immigrants to the original Hawaiian version of fish and coconut milk.

---

4 firm, white fish fillets (cod, haddock, etc.)
1 small onion, peeled and cut in 8 wedges
2 tbsp peanut oil
2 tomatoes, skinned, de-seeded and diced
1 red or green pepper, seeded and cut in eighths
1 1/2 tbsp fresh chopped basil, or 1/2 tsp dried
1 fresh hot red chili pepper, de-seeded and finely chopped
(or a good pinch of dried chili pepper)
salt and pepper
1 1/2 cups coconut milk

Preheat oven to 350°F. In a baking dish, arrange the fish in a single layer. Separate the onion wedges into layers. Heat the peanut oil in a frying pan. Add onion and fry until transparent. Add tomato, red or green pepper, basil, chili, salt, and pepper. Fry for five minutes, stirring. Add the coconut milk. Heat until just warm. Pour the vegetable-coconut mixture over the fish. Cover dish. Bake for 20–30 minutes or until fish is flaky.

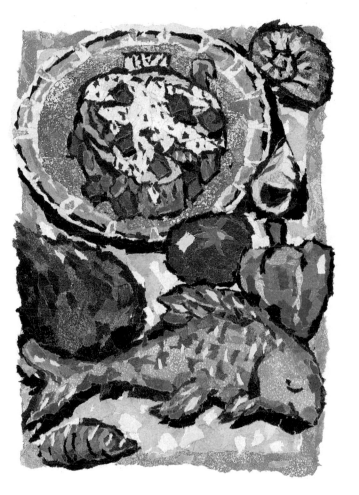

Laulau

Originally cooked in a barbecue pit and served at *luaus*, *laulaus* are now served at fast-food restaurants all over the Islands. We first tried them on the island of Kauai. The restaurant owner roasted them in an underground *imu* (oven) behind her diner.

The rich pork and the salty fish cooked in the tangy-sweet greens is an unforgettable combination. To simulate the smoky flavor of *laulau* cooked in the ground, toss some wood chips into the water used for steaming.

8–16 wrapping-leaves: frozen banana leaves (available in some Asian markets), Swiss chard leaves or spinach leaves
1/2 lb salted butterfish or black cod or
any firm white fish, cut into 8 pieces
1/4 lb boneless pork butt, cut into 1/2 inch cubes
1/2 cup trimmed green onion, cut into rings
(makes 8 laulaus)

Set out 1 large banana leaf, or 2 overlapping Swiss chard or spinach leaves per *laulau*. In the center of the leaves, place the fish, pork, and onion. Wrap up into a compact bundle. Tie with thin string. Place in a steamer and steam for one hour. Remove string and serve hot.

Chinese Chicken Wings

The rich, sweet-and-sour flavors of Chinese Chicken Wings make them a perfect complement to fruity Hawaiian cocktails. The sauce is equally good on spare-ribs, chicken, or vegetable kebabs.

---

2 cloves garlic, peeled and crushed
2 green onions, trimmed and chopped
1/4 cup soy sauce
1 tbsp sherry
1/2 cup water
1/3 cup sugar
12 chicken wings
3 tbsp oyster sauce (available in Asian markets)

In a small saucepan, combine all ingredients except chicken. Bring to a boil, then simmer for 1 hour. Meanwhile, cut off the tips of the chicken wings. Cut each wing through the joint into two pieces. Place wings on a baking sheet. Baste chicken with sauce and grill, turning once, until brown, crisp, and cooked through. Serve with a side dish of sauce for dipping, if liked.

Lumpia

Although their food is not the most prevalent on the Islands, the Filipinos are an integral part of Hawaii's culinary heritage. *Lumpia* is their version of the Chinese egg roll and has numerous variations.

---

1 tbsp corn oil
4 cloves garlic, peeled and crushed
1 small onion, finely chopped
3 tsp grated fresh ginger root
1 medium carrot, cut into match-stick strips
1 cup bean sprouts
1 cup slivered green beans
8 oz shredded pork
3 tbsp soy sauce
1 fresh red chili, seeded and finely chopped (or a good pinch dried)
salt and pepper
4 lumpia or egg roll wrappers
2 egg yolks, slightly beaten
oil for frying

Heat the tablespoon of oil in a frying pan. Fry garlic and onion and ginger root until softened. Add prepared vegetable and pork. Fry quickly for 2 minutes, stirring so that cooked vegetables remain crisp. Add soy sauce, chili, and seasoning to taste. Drain and allow to cool. In the center of a *lumpia* wrapper or sheet of filo pastry, folded in half, place $1/4$ of the filling, tuck in the two ends and roll. Brush egg yolk on all the seams. In a heavy pan or deep fat fryer, heat oil to 375°F (or until a cube of day-old bread browns in 30 seconds) and deep fry until golden. Drain on kitchen towels. Serve with soy, *teriyaki*, (see page 11) or red chili pepper sauce.

Korean Barbecued Beef

The Mongols brought beef to Korea and it has played an important part in the Korean diet ever since. In Hawaii, Korean barbecue restaurants abound and beckon hungry tourists and locals alike with the smoky aroma of wood-charred, garlicky ribs. The marinade is equally good for grilling cuts of pork or beef.

---

1 ½ lbs rump or sirloin steak, cut into 4 pieces
¼ cup soy sauce
3 tbsp sesame oil
4 tbsp tahini or sesame seed paste
2 tbsp sugar
1 small onion, peeled and finely chopped
2 green onions, trimmed and finely chopped
2 cloves garlic, peeled and crushed
¼ inch piece fresh ginger root, peeled and grated
salt and pepper

In a shallow baking pan, arrange the steaks in a single layer. Combine remaining ingredients in a small bowl. Pour over meat and leave to marinate for 1-3 hours. Grill or barbecue steaks, turning once, until cooked (about 3-4 minutes for rare, 7-8 minutes for well done on each side). Serve meat with *kim chee* (see page 35).

Oven Kalua Pig

This is an at-home version of the pit-roasted variety served at *luaus*. The traditional pig is cleaned, filled with rock salt, seasonings, and hot rocks, wrapped in a basket, lowered into a banana leaf-lined, heated *imu* (roasting pit), then covered with banana leaves, stones, and earth.

At one time only men were allowed to eat roasted pig. Women were not allowed to eat pork until 1819 when King Liholiho left the men's feast to dine on fish and *poi* with the women. With this recipe, you can get the traditional pit-roasted flavor by using liquid smoke.

---

1 ¹/₂ tbsp rock salt
3 tbsp soy sauce
1 scant tsp Worcestershire sauce
2 cloves garlic, peeled and crushed
4 inch piece fresh ginger root peeled and grated
2 tsp liquid smoke (optional)
3 lb joint pork roast (boneless shoulder or leg)
(serves 8)

Preheat the oven to 325°F. In a small bowl, mix together salt, soy sauce, Worcestershire sauce, garlic, ginger root, and liquid smoke (if using). Rub pork with the mixture, allow to stand 1 hour. Wrap the pork in foil. Place in a roasting pan and roast for 3-4 hours or until very tender. Unwrap and carve or shred meat.

Chicken Long Rice

Long rice is not a grain, but long thin noodles made from mung bean flour, most likely brought to Hawaii by the Chinese plantation laborers. A delicious main dish, no two recipes for it are the same; anything goes. Try adding chopped tomatoes, mushrooms, or five-spice powder. Experiment with chopped green onions or hard-boiled eggs as garnishes.

---

3 lb oven-ready chicken
$1/2$ inch piece fresh ginger root, peeled and sliced
1 tbsp salt
2 cloves garlic, peeled and crushed
1 onion, peeled and sliced
2 tbsp vegetable or peanut oil
12 oz Chinese mung bean noodles or sai fun noodles
(available at Asian markets) — or egg noodles
2 tbsp soy sauce
$1/2$ bunch green onions, trimmed and sliced in rings

In a large saucepan, place the chicken and enough water to cover. Add ginger root and salt. Cover and cook over a moderate heat until chicken is tender, about 1 hour. Leave chicken to cool in the cooking liquid. When cold, remove the chicken. Bone and cut the meat into $1/2$ inch cubes, discarding skin. Strain and reserve cooking liquid.

In a separate large pan, fry the garlic and onion in oil for 2 minutes. Add the noodles and just enough of the reserved cooking liquid to cover. Add the soy and the chicken (plus any of the optional ingredients mentioned above: tomatoes, mushrooms, etc.) and simmer for five minutes until noodles are cooked. Garnish with the green onions and serve.

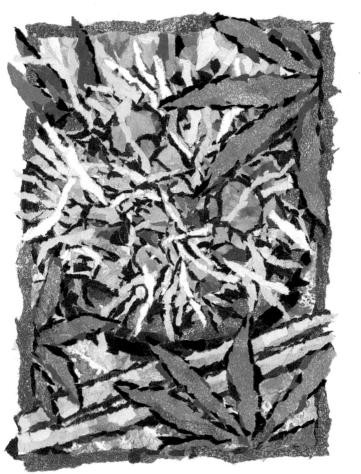

Portuguese Bean Soup

This hearty soup, brought to Hawaii by immigrants from Madeira and the Azores, is standard fare in island homes and restaurants. It makes an ample meal served with tossed green salad, a crusty loaf, and a crisp, dry, white wine.

---

6 oz pink beans or red kidney beans, soaked
6 oz cannellini beans, soaked
6 tbsp olive oil
1 onion, peeled and chopped
3 cloves garlic, peeled and crushed
3 Portuguese sausages (linguica), chopped
(or chorizo or Italian sausage)
2 carrots, peeled and diced
2 potatoes, peeled and finely diced
14 oz can tomatoes
1 tsp dried thyme
salt and pepper
2 pt chicken stock, home-made or made with 3 stock cubes
2 cups, chopped kale, Swiss chard,
or spinach, well washed
dash of red wine vinegar
1 bunch parsley, finely chopped
(serves 4-6)

Drain beans, place in separate pans, bring to a boil and boil rapidly for 10 minutes. Drain. Add fresh boiling water to cover and simmer until beans are tender — about 50 minutes. Drain, reserving liquid. In a large pan, heat 3 tablespoons olive oil, fry onions, garlic, and sausage until onions are transparent, about 15 minutes. Add carrots, potatoes, tomatoes, thyme, salt, pepper, beans, and chicken stock. Bring to a boil. Reduce heat and simmer for 45 minutes to an hour (adding reserved bean liquid if necessary). Meanwhile, in a frying pan, heat remaining olive oil and fry the kale until limp, stirring continuously. Add to soup. During the last five minutes of cooking, add vinegar and parsley. Serve hot.

Chinese Spicy Eggplant

The Chinese do not eat dairy products and meat is used only to add flavor as it is scarce and too expensive for many. The following vegetable dish is a Chinese restaurant staple in Hawaii and is made with the locally grown long eggplant. This is often picked when still green, so when cooked, has a firm, meaty consistency.

1 cup peanut or vegetable oil	4 cloves garlic, peeled and crushed
1 lb eggplant (preferably Japanese) sliced into 1 inch strips	1 tsp sugar
	1 tsp cornstarch or arrowroot
1 cup finely diced pork or chicken	2 tbsp soy sauce
1 1/4 tsp red chili, chopped, fresh, or 1/4 tsp dried chili	1 1/4 tsp white vinegar
1 inch piece fresh ginger root, peeled and grated	

In a skillet or wok, heat oil. Add eggplant and fry, stirring until brown. Drain on kitchen towels, blotting excess oil. Add meat to skillet. Fry, stirring, until cooked, then remove with a draining spoon. Pour out oil. In a small bowl, blend remaining ingredients and add to pan. Add meat and eggplant. Stir together over medium heat until hot. Serve.

Manapua

Manapua is the same as *char siu bao*, the steamed pork buns of Chinese *dim sum*. In Hawaii, these fist-sized pillows of dough filled with sweet and spicy roasted meat are the ideal fast food to be eaten at the beach or on-the-run.

Filling:	Dough:
1 tbsp cornstarch	1 3/4 cups warm water
2 tbsp sugar	2 1/2 tsp active dry yeast (1 package)
1 tbsp soy sauce	1/2 cup sugar
3/4 cup water	1 tbsp vegetable oil
1 lb char siu, diced (see below)	1 tsp salt
2 tbsp green onions, chopped	5 1/2 cups flour
(makes 12)	

To prepare filling, thoroughly mix cornstarch, sugar, soy sauce, and water in a saucepan and boil, stirring constantly. Lower heat and simmer until thickened (about 1 minute). Remove from heat, allow to cool, then add *char siu* and green onions.

To make dough, add the yeast and the sugar to the warm water, mixing slowly until completely dissolved. Stir in the oil and salt. Add the flour a little at a time, stirring as you go, until the dough is workable. Knead by hand for 5 minutes, adding flour if dough becomes too sticky. Place a small amount of vegetable oil in a bowl and turn the kneaded dough in the bowl until lightly oiled. Cover bowl with a clean kitchen towel and leave in a warm spot for the dough to rise until doubled in volume (about 90 minutes). Punch down the dough, break into 12 pieces, form into balls then flatten into 3-inch circles. Place a small amount of filling at the center of each circle, gather up edges and pinch at top to close completely.

Turn pinched side down onto a lightly oiled baking tray, cover with a clean towel, and let rise until doubled (about 45 minutes). Place on a rack above (not in) boiling water and steam, covered, for 25 minutes or until dough is cooked. Serve immediately with extra soy sauce for dipping.

Char Siu

Chinese roasted pork tenderloin — *char siu* — is simple and elegant when sliced in thin rounds and served with hot mustard and toasted sesame seeds for dipping. *Char siu* is also the tasty, central ingredient in island-style *manapua*.

---

³/₄ cup soy sauce	3 slices of fresh ginger
¹/₄ cup sake	3 garlic cloves, crushed
¹/₂ cup sugar	3 lb pork fillet
1 tsp Chinese five-spice powder	

Combine first six ingredients and marinate pork, refrigerated, overnight. Bake at 350°F for 90 minutes or until meat appears white at the center, but is still juicy. Allow to cool, slice thinly, and serve.

Cucumber-Carrot Namasu

Japanese immigrants brought *namasu* to Hawaii. Use it as a refreshing relish with chicken and fish or serve it as a side dish or salad at picnics and barbecues.

1 Japanese (or English) cucumber, thinly sliced
1/4 tsp salt
1/2 medium carrot, peeled and thinly sliced
3/4 cup Japanese rice vinegar
(or half white wine vinegar, half water)
3 tbsp superfine sugar
1/2 tsp grated, peeled fresh ginger root

In a medium mixing bowl, drizzle half the salt over the cucumber. Leave for 20 minutes. Squeeze to remove liquid. Add carrots. In a small mixing bowl, mix vinegar, sugar, ginger, and remaining salt. Add mixture to vegetables. Chill before serving.

Kim Chee

The tart, garlicky flavor of *kim chee* is a perfect accompaniment to Korean barbecued meat. The Koreans pickle this relish in crocks and bury them underground. The crocks are placed in the earth in the autumn and removed in the spring when the ground softens. This recipe approximates the intense flavors which result from the six-month fermentation. Make plenty: you may become addicted to this fiery hot relish, like many residents of Hawaii.

1 medium green cabbage
1/4 cup rock salt
1 cup water
1 tsp salt
2 inch piece fresh ginger root, peeled and grated

1 onion, cut in half and sliced in thin rings
8 cloves garlic, peeled and crushed
5 red chilies, de-seeded, and finely chopped (or 3 tsp red dried)

Quarter cabbage, remove stump, then slice thinly. Place cabbage in a large mixing bowl. Sprinkle with rock salt. Pour water over cabbage. Let stand for 1 1/2–2 hours, stirring occasionally. Drain and squeeze out excess water. Put cabbage back in the mixing bowl and add the remaining ingredients. Spoon *kim chee* into a clean screw-top jar and cover with lid. Put in a warm place for 24 hours then store in the refrigerator for up to 3 months, adding white vinegar to cover cabbage if liquid evaporates.

Note: You can also make cucumber *kim chee*, by substituting thinly sliced cucumber for cabbage. Sprinkle coarsely grated cucumbers with rock salt, then rinse with water after 1 hour and continue as with cabbage recipe.

Coconut Milk and Coconut Cream

Experiment with coconut milk by substituting it for cow's milk in your favorite recipes. Coconut milk lends a rich, sweet flavor to curries and puddings and an exotic, Polynesian touch when poured over sweet potatoes or baked bananas. Or use it as the Hawaiians do — as a stock in which to bake chicken and fish.

To make coconut milk:
3 cups fresh grated or unsweetened desiccated coconut
1 1/2 cups boiling coconut water or tap water

Put grated coconut in a bowl. Pour boiling coconut or tap water over. Let it stand for 20 minutes. Purée coconut and water in a food processor or blender. Strain through cheesecloth.

Note: To make coconut cream, use 1/3-1/2 cup of boiling coconut water or tap water, then follow the directions for coconut milk.

Sesame Salad Dressing

A Hawaiian combination of Eastern flavors and European preparations, this dressing is delicious on rice, pasta, and green salads or as a marinade.

$1/4$ cup soy sauce
$3/4$ cup rice vinegar
$1/2$ cup red wine vinegar
I tbsp superfine sugar
$1/2$ inch piece fresh ginger root, peeled and grated
2 cloves garlic, peeled and crushed
salt and pepper
$2^{1}/4$ cups corn or peanut oil
$1/4$ cup roasted sesame seed oil
(makes 2 pints)

In a food processor or a mixing bowl, blend all ingredients except the oils. Then, in a slow steady steam, pour the oils through the feed tube while running the machine or into the mixing bowl. If you are making the dressing by hand, whisk the entire time you are adding the oil. The dressing can be stored in the refrigerator for up to three weeks.

Papaya Seed Dressing

The sweetness of this dressing works especially well with dark salad greens such as watercress and spinach. If you can't get papaya, use the alternatives suggested, but nothing can replicate the subtle quality of this tropical fruit.

---

³/₄ cup papaya or orange juice
¹/₄ cup fresh lemon or lime juice
¹/₄ cup white wine vinegar
3 shallots, peeled and finely chopped
2 tbsp superfine sugar
salt and pepper
3 cups corn oil
1¹/₂ cups papaya seeds, coarsely ground
or ¹/₄ cup poppy seeds
(makes 4³/₄ cups)

In a food processor or a mixing bowl, blend all ingredients except the oil and seeds. In a slow steady steam, pour the oil through the feed tube while running the machine or into the mixing bowl. If you are making the dressing by hand, whisk the entire time you are adding the oil. Add either ground papaya seeds or poppy seeds. The dressing can be stored in the refrigerator for up to 3 days.

Hawaiian Sweet Potato Casserole

The Samoans baked fruit and vegetables in coconut milk and may have been the originators of this recipe, with its many variations. This is one of our favorite versions in which the Southeast Asian touch of mint and European brandy or Caribbean rum are added to the basic dish of potatoes, fruit, and coconut milk.

---

1 tbsp butter
4 large sweet potatoes, peeled, parboiled and sliced
4 bananas, peeled and sliced
4 apples, peeled, cored, and sliced in rings
1 1/2 cups coconut milk (see page 36)
1/2 cup brandy or rum
2 tbsp fresh mint, chopped

Preheat oven to 350°F. Grease a large, shallow casserole dish with butter. Layer sweet potatoes, bananas, and apples. In a small bowl, blend coconut milk, brandy, and mint. Pour over casserole. Cover and bake for about 30 minutes. Uncover dish for the last 10 minutes of cooking to brown.

Kona Coffee and Cream Shave Ice

Hawaiian shave ice is a crushed ice and syrup dessert served in paper cones. It is sold by seaside vendors whose trucks and storefronts are emblazoned with images of the syrupy sweet cones painted in neon rainbow colors. Ours is a sophisticated version which features a Kona coffee base and is designed for adult after-dinner fare.

The Kona Coast, on the island of Hawaii, is the home of the Kona coffee plantations — the only plantations in Hawaii or the United States where coffee is commercially grown. The excellence of the beans is attributed to Kona's ideal coastal climate. Kona coffee is available worldwide but any fresh ground coffee will work well.

---

4 cups sugar
2 cups water
2 cups Kona coffee, brewed triple-strength
$^1/_2$ cup evaporated milk
$^1/_3$ cup coffee liqueur (or mix half coffee liqueur
and half macadamia liqueur)
crushed ice

Boil the sugar and water in a saucepan for 5 minutes. Cool. Add the coffee, evaporated milk, and liqueur. Remove from heat. Spoon crushed ice into 4 dessert dishes or glasses and pour the syrup over. Serve with a spoon and a straw.

Mocha Macadamia Nut Brownies

At the turn of the century, twenty years after the smooth-shelled macadamia nut was introduced to Hawaii, the Agricultural Experiment Station distributed macadamia seeds to Kona Coast coffee growers. Coffee and macadamia not only grow well together, but are delicious when combined in desserts.

Getting to the nuts is not always an easy matter; the shells are hard to crack. While a rock or hammer works, a favorite contemporary Hawaiian method is to put the nuts under a board and back over them with a car. For a simpler solution, buy the shelled variety!

---

butter for greasing
7 tbsp unsalted butter, cut into pieces
4 ozs unsweetened chocolate, finely chopped
³/₄ cup sugar
2 eggs, at room temperature
1 tsp vanilla extract
¹/₂ cup all-purpose flour
1 tbsp instant coffee powder
good pinch of salt
2 oz macadamia nuts, toasted and coarsely chopped
(makes 12 brownies)

Preheat oven to 350°F. Lightly butter and flour an 8-inch square baking pan. Melt unsalted butter in a medium saucepan over low heat. Remove from heat and add chocolate. Allow to stand for 1 minute then whisk until smooth. Allow to stand for 10 minutes. Whisk in sugar. Whisk in eggs, one at a time, then vanilla.

Using a wooden spoon, stir in flour, coffee and salt, until just blended. Stir in macadamia nuts. Spread batter evenly into prepared pan and bake in the center of oven for 25 minutes, until a toothpick inserted in the center comes out with a moist crumb. Cool on a wired rack and cut into squares.

Haupia

Coconut Pudding

Haupia is a traditional *luau* dish. Today, it is most often chilled in a rectangular cake pan, cut into squares and served on a *ti* leaf. We like to make it in ramekin dishes because it is easier to eat and we can add tropical toppings to enhance the flavor.

---

3 tbsp cornstarch
4 tbsp superfine sugar
1²/₃ cups coconut milk (see page 36)
²/₃ cup grated, fresh or unsweetened desiccated coconut
¹/₂ tsp vanilla extract
butter for greasing
(serves 6)

In a small mixing bowl, blend cornstarch, sugar and ¹/₄ cup coconut milk. In a medium saucepan, bring remaining coconut milk to a boil. Slowly add cornstarch mixture, stirring constantly until mixture thickens. Cool. Add coconut and vanilla. Stir. Pour into buttered ramekin dishes and chill before serving.

Note: For variety, you can top this dessert with crushed pineapple, chopped papaya, or chocolate sauce and chopped macadamia nuts.

Banana Poi

No experience of Hawaiian food is complete without a sampling of
poi. A healthful staple of the Polynesian diet, tart and starchy taro
poi, is rarely made in the contemporary Hawaiian home. The taro
"corms" must be peeled and cooked carefully (taro contains crystals
of calcium oxalate which, if the root is not cooked properly, become
painful irritants to the mouth and throat), then pounded with water
into a smooth paste. More frequently, taro *poi* is purchased in
color-coded plastic bags from the grocery store. A statewide
shortage of the taro for making *poi* has made even the prepared
variety difficult to come by. A delicious and simple alternative is
banana *poi,* a Samoan contribution to Hawaiian cuisine. Banana *poi*
is sweeter and creamier than the *poi* made from pounded taro root,
and can be served as a cold side dish or dessert.

---

2 cups very ripe bananas, peeled
1 cup coconut cream (see page 36)
2 tbsp lime juice

In a food processor or in a mixing bowl, using a potato masher or
fork, mash the bananas to a smooth paste. Stirring constantly, slowly
add the coconut cream and lime juice until well blended. Chill before
serving.

Banana Macadamia Bread

When the early Polynesians migrated to Hawaii, they probably brought banana plants with them — the starchy, cooking bananas that now grow wild in the valleys of Hawaii. Later, in the nineteenth century, sweeter Brazilian and Chinese varieties were introduced to the Islands. This recipe for banana bread uses the more recently introduced, sweeter variety.

1 cup mashed bananas	1/2 tsp bicarbonate of soda
1 tbsp rum	2/3 cup superfine sugar
2 cups all-purpose flour	1/3 cup butter
2 1/2 tsp baking powder	2 eggs
1/2 tsp salt	1 cup macadamia nuts,
1/2 tsp allspice	coarsely chopped

Preheat oven to 350°F. In a medium-size bowl, mash bananas and rum. In another medium bowl, sift flour, baking powder, salt, allspice and soda together. In a medium mixing bowl, beat sugar and butter until creamy. Add eggs one at a time, beating well after each addition. Add flour mixture a little at a time until mixed in well. Slowly add banana mixture, beating after each addition until smooth. Add nuts. Pour mixture into a greased 8 inch x 4 inch x 3 inch loaf pan. Bake about one hour, until firm and a toothpick inserted in center comes out clean.

For a less expensive variation, use walnuts or hazelnuts instead of macadamias.

Malasadas

These puffs of sugary, crisp fried dough are a gift to Hawaii from its Portuguese population. More airy than American doughnuts, *malasadas* can be bought by the bag from neighborhood sellers or at stalls during local Hawaiian festivals where they're served fried and rolled in cane sugar before your eyes.

1/2 pkg dried yeast	1/4 tsp vanilla extract
1/2 tsp superfine sugar	1/3 cup butter, melted
2 tbsp hand-hot water	1/2 cup evaporated milk
3 eggs, beaten	1/2 cup water
3 cups all-purpose flour	1/2 tsp salt
good pinch of nutmeg	oil for frying
1/4 tsp cinnamon	1 cup superfine sugar for coating

(makes 36)

In a small bowl, dissolve yeast and sugar in water. Leave for 10 minutes in a warm place until frothy. Sift flour into a large mixing bowl. Make a well in the center and add the yeast mixture, eggs, and remaining ingredients except oil and sugar for coating. Beat until mixture forms a smooth dough. Cover and put in a warm place until doubled in bulk. Punch back, cover, and let rise again. In a deep fat fryer, heat oil to 375°F or until a cube of day-old bread browns in 30 seconds. Spoon dough, 1 teaspoon at a time, into oil. Fry until brown. Drain on kitchen paper then roll in granulated or superfine sugar. Serve hot.

Fresh Pineapple

Over the years, the pineapple has been associated with Hawaii more than any other tropical fruit. It is believed that pineapples were brought from South America by the Spanish and became big business when it was subsequently cultivated on plantations for canning and shipping. It can also be found growing wild in the hills. The pineapple is actually a cluster of small fruits. When the plant is flowering, each fruit blossoms, creating a magnificent cluster.

If your pineapple tastes a bit too tart, try a dash of salt rather than sugar to sweeten — a trick we learned in the 1960s on a cannery tour.

---

1 ripe pineapple
8 sprigs fresh mint, chopped

There is an art to peeling, coring, and cutting the pineapple. Peel the rind from top to bottom with a paring knife. Cut diagonal grooves around the pineapple to remove eyes. Cut off the top and slice fruit into rounds. Remove the core from each slice. Place slices on a plate and sprinkle with mint.

Drinks

On a balmy Hawaiian day, it is essential to stay cool. One way is to head down to the beach and another is to treat yourself to some tropical refreshment. Here are two drinks guaranteed to do the trick. But be careful with the rum-laced "Mai Tai" — it's an infamous cocktail known to catch many a tourist by surprise!

Tropical Fruit Punch

I lemon, squeezed	I cup orange juice
I lime, squeezed	superfine sugar to taste
¹/₂ cup guava	I cup soda water
or mango nectar	star fruit, cut into 4 slices
I cup	mint sprigs
pineapple juice	

Combine juice of lemon and lime with other juices and sugar to taste. Chill. Serve topped up with soda water in tall glasses with lots of ice, garnished with a star fruit slice and a sprig of mint.

Mai Tai

¹/₄ oz lime juice	¹/₄ oz orange curaçao
¹/₄ oz lemon juice	¹/₂ oz light rum
¹/₂ oz orgeat or	4 oz pineapple juice
grenadine syrup	¹/₂ oz dark rum
(makes I cocktail)	

Pour first six ingredients over ice in a wide, short glass. Finish with a float of dark rum and a paper umbrella, just for fun.

Index